A Ladybird Bible Book

Moses
and Joshua

Text by Jenny Robertson
Illustrations by Alan Parry

Scripture Union/Ladybird

A long line of people made their way across the desert – the Hebrew people were leaving Egypt. For longer than anyone could remember they

had been kept there as slaves, but now they were free. God had rescued them. The people knew that God was still with them, looking after them on their long journey to the new land he promised to give them, but they only grumbled.

'Why did you take us away from Egypt?' they complained to their leader, Moses. 'At least we had enough to eat there! We'll die of hunger and thirst here in the desert!'

'God rescued you from Egypt,' Moses reminded them. 'He can give us food even out here. Why don't you trust him?'

Next morning the earth was covered with something thin and flaky like frost. 'Gather it before it melts,' Moses told them. 'Collect what you need but no more. It is the food that God has provided.'

The people hurried to pick it up. It tasted like honey biscuits, and they called it 'manna'. They all had as much as they wanted; God gave them manna to eat every day while they were in the desert.

The Hebrews journeyed southwards through the desert for many months until they came to a mountain called Sinai. They set up camp at its foot, and Moses climbed up the mountain alone to pray.

There God spoke to him: 'I promise to lead you all and look after you. I have chosen you for my own people and you must obey my laws.'

Moses went back and told the people what God had said. 'You must prepare yourselves to worship God,' he added. The people followed

him up the mountain. A cloud covered Sinai. Thunder rumbled. Lightning and fire flashed and smoke billowed low. A trumpet peal sounded, and the people trembled. 'The Lord God is here,' they whispered.

God spoke to Moses again. He gave him laws for the people to keep, so that they would behave in a way that pleased him. Moses told everyone what God had said. Then he went back up the mountain. This time he took one of his captains with him, a young man called Joshua.

Moses and Joshua were away for a long time and the people grew frightened. 'Moses' God has taken him away. Let's choose a different god.' And they begged Aaron, Moses' brother, to make them one. Aaron was frightened of the people, so he agreed. He collected their gold jewellery and melted it down. Then he made a statue of a bull from the hot gold. Everyone cheered and held a great feast in honour of the new god, although it was only lifeless metal.

By now, Moses and Joshua were on their way back. Moses carried two heavy slabs of stone on which God himself had written the new laws. They were surprised to hear singing and shouting in the camp. Then Moses saw the golden statue, and he was furious.

'God chose you to be his people. You promised not to make statues and worship them instead of God!' he shouted.

He smashed the stone slabs with God's laws to the ground. Then he melted down the statue and prayed for the people. 'Forgive them, Lord God,' he begged.

'I don't break my promises,' said God. 'Cut two new slabs of stone like the ones you broke, and I will give the people their laws again.'

Moses kept the new stone slabs in a special box covered with gold, and God told the people to make a beautiful tent to protect it when they set up camp. God himself would surround the tent in a special way, so it was to be called 'the tent of God's Presence'.

The people all gave what they could to make the tent. Some brought wood for the tentpoles. Others gave their jewellery. Weavers brought fine linen, woven with coloured threads, while

others brought coarser cloth made of goat's hair, fine leather and rams' hides dyed scarlet. They brought spices and oil for the lamp inside the tent. Then skilled craftsmen set to work to sew the cloth together, to make rings and fastenings, and put up the tent. When it was ready a cloud touched it and a dazzling light shone through it. The people saw that God was with them. They fell on their faces and worshipped him.

At last they left Mount Sinai and went on with their journey. The way was very hard and they began to miss the green fields around the River Nile in Egypt. 'We used to have cucumbers and water-melons, onions, leeks and garlic to eat,' they said. 'We had fish, too. Now we've nothing except manna. If only we could get some meat for a change!'

Moses overheard, and he was angry. 'Why did you get me to look after these ungrateful people?' he asked God. 'Where am I supposed

to find meat for them all? I can't cope with their whining any more!'

'Moses; you need some helpers,' God said. 'I will choose leaders to help you, and I'll give everyone enough meat for a month!'

God did exactly as he promised. He chose seventy leaders to help Moses look after the tribes. Then a strong wind carried flocks of little birds called quails into the camp. The birds were tired, and it was easy for the people to catch them. That night everyone had meat for supper.

Then they set off again, travelling towards the country of Canaan, the land God had promised them. Moses sent out spies to find out what sort of people lived there – fierce fighting men or wandering tribes.

The spies returned with news. They brought a bunch of grapes so heavy it needed two men to carry it.

'Look!' they said, 'We picked these grapes, and figs and pomegranates, too. The land is very good, but the people are fierce and live in big cities with strong walls. We even saw giants there who made us feel like tiny grasshoppers!'

'Let's choose another leader and go back to Egypt!' everyone exclaimed in terror.

But Joshua, Moses' helper, who had gone with the spies, cried, 'Don't be silly! God is fighting for us. He will help us conquer the land, giants and all!'

Another spy, called Caleb, agreed with Joshua but the people refused to listen.

Suddenly a bright light shone from the tent, and God spoke. 'The people still don't trust me! Not one of them shall cross into the Promised Land except for Caleb and Joshua. They must go on wandering through the desert until they die. Then I shall give the land to their children.'

Sadly the Hebrews set off from the edge of the Promised Land, back into the desert.

In spite of everything it wasn't long before they were grumbling again. They came to a place where there was no water, and, instead of asking God to help them, they complained to Moses.

He took Aaron with him to the Tent of the Presence to pray. Then they called everyone together in front of a huge rock.

Moses struck it twice with his stick. Water spouted out, sparkling in the sunlight. Full of wonder the people crowded round and drank.

Moses did not tell them it was God who made the water pour out of the rock. He hadn't been true to God, and now he, too, would not be able to enter the Promised Land.

On their long journey the Hebrews crossed land belonging to many different tribes. Moses would send messengers to the ruler of each place explaining that they wanted to travel peacefully across his land, without taking any food or water. Often, though, the ruler would meet them with an army, and then the Hebrews had to fight their way through.

A fierce king, called Og, heard that they were coming and set out to attack them. Og was a huge man, the last of the tribe known as the giants, but the Hebrews were experienced fighters by now.

'God is on our side,' Joshua encouraged them. They defeated King Og and his army and captured his towns.

God gave them victory over everyone who tried to stop them. The years went by, and the people who had refused to trust God died. At last it was time to go into the Promised Land. Moses led the people to the banks of the River Jordan. On the other side lay their new country.

By now Aaron was dead and Moses was a very old man. He longed to lead the people into their new land, but he knew that God had said 'no'.

Then God spoke to him again. 'Climb that mountain and you will be able to see what the Promised Land, Canaan, is like.'

So Moses climbed the mountain. Brown desert hills rose sharply around him, but beyond the River Jordan shimmered the green valleys and hills of Canaan. Moses' eyesight was still good. He could see it all clearly. It was a good land!

He went back to the camp singing God's praises. There he reminded everyone of the laws they had promised to obey. Finally he blessed them all.

'No other nation is as blessed as you, because God has chosen you and he will keep you safe,' he said.

Then Moses died. The people were sad. They never forgot him.

'No one is greater than Moses, because the Lord spoke to him face to face,' they said.

Joshua, Moses' helper, became the new leader. At once he began to make plans for capturing Canaan. The first step was to take the enemies' town of Jericho with its high, double walls. Joshua sent two spies across the Jordan. They slipped secretly into Jericho.

They met a woman called Rahab who invited them to stay in her house, perched between the walls. Someone spotted them and told the king, who sent his soldiers to the house. Rahab saw them coming and hid the spies on her flat roof under bundles of flax.

Soon the soldiers were pounding on her door. 'Bring out those spies!' they yelled.

'What spies?' asked Rahab. 'Some men called by earlier, but they left the city when the gates shut at sunset. If you hurry you might catch them.'

Rahab laughed as she heard the gates open to let the soldiers out. She helped the spies escape from her window down the high outer wall.

'I'm doing this because I believe that your God is the true God,' she said. 'We have heard how he has helped you win battles, and the whole town is terrified. Promise you won't kill me or any of my family when you capture Jericho.'

The spies promised and gave her a red cord to mark her house. Then they hurried back to Joshua.

'Everyone is terrified of us! God will help us win a tremendous victory!' they declared.

First they had to cross the River Jordan. They stared at the water, wondering how they would get across. Joshua called them together.

'God will help us,' he said. 'When you see the priests going down to the river carrying the gold box with the laws in it, follow them with all your belongings.'

The people did as Joshua said. When the priests stepped into the water the river stopped flowing; the water piled up to the north and dry land appeared.

Everyone crossed over safely. They chose twelve large stones from the river bed and set them up on the bank to remind everyone how they had crossed the river. Then they camped. For the first time there was no manna for them to eat. From now on they could eat the food of Canaan.

When the king of Jericho saw that the Hebrews were camping so close to the city he barred and bolted all the gates. Sentries guarded them, and no one was allowed to go in or out. One day Joshua was walking alone beside the city when he noticed a man standing in front of him, holding an unsheathed sword.

'Are you one of our soldiers or an enemy?' Joshua challenged him.

'I am the commander of the army of the Lord God,' the stranger answered.

Joshua bowed his face to the ground. 'I am your servant. Give me your orders, Commander.'

'Take off your sandals. This is holy ground.' Joshua obeyed. Now he knew for sure that they would capture the town. God told Joshua exactly what to do.

The Hebrews didn't storm the walls or batter down the gates. Instead they marched round the city; first a guard of soldiers, then seven priests blowing their trumpets, then more priests carrying the precious box, and the army tramping behind in silence. They did the same thing for seven days, while the people of Jericho laughed and jeered at them from their high walls.

On the seventh day they marched seven times, right round the walls. Then Joshua yelled: 'God has given us the city!' and the people cheered and blew their trumpets.

At once the houses and towers along the wall began to topple. With a loud rumble the walls smashed down, and the Hebrews poured into Jericho, yelling and cheering. They found Rahab and her family and led them safely out of their ruined home, but they destroyed the rest of the city.

The news spread like wildfire. Soon Joshua and the Hebrews were feared all over Canaan. They began to capture the rest of the land and settle in the country that God had given them.

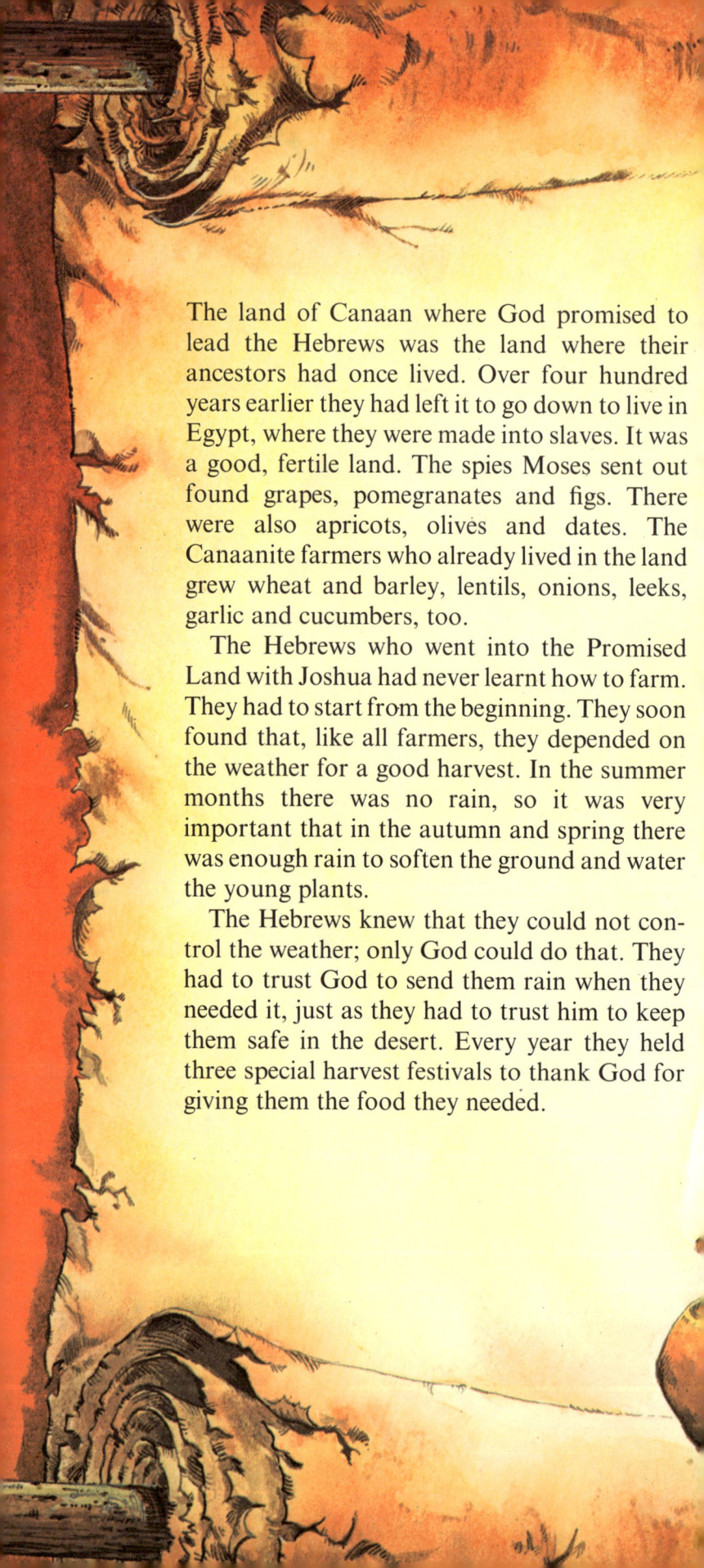

The land of Canaan where God promised to lead the Hebrews was the land where their ancestors had once lived. Over four hundred years earlier they had left it to go down to live in Egypt, where they were made into slaves. It was a good, fertile land. The spies Moses sent out found grapes, pomegranates and figs. There were also apricots, olives and dates. The Canaanite farmers who already lived in the land grew wheat and barley, lentils, onions, leeks, garlic and cucumbers, too.

The Hebrews who went into the Promised Land with Joshua had never learnt how to farm. They had to start from the beginning. They soon found that, like all farmers, they depended on the weather for a good harvest. In the summer months there was no rain, so it was very important that in the autumn and spring there was enough rain to soften the ground and water the young plants.

The Hebrews knew that they could not control the weather; only God could do that. They had to trust God to send them rain when they needed it, just as they had to trust him to keep them safe in the desert. Every year they held three special harvest festivals to thank God for giving them the food they needed.